THE WEAPONS ENCYCLOPÆDIA
TANK AIRCRAFT AFV SHIP ARTILLERY VEHICLES SECRET WEAPON

TWE-037 ENG

LIGHT TANK TYPE 95 HA-GO AND DERIVATIVES

THE WEAPONS ENCYCLOPAEDIA

EDITORIAL STAFF
Luca Cristini, Paolo Crippa.

ACADEMIC STAFF
Enrico Acerbi, Massimiliano Afiero, Aldo Antonicelli, Ruggero Calò, Luigi Carretta, Flavio Chistè, Anna Cristini, Carlo Cucut, Salvo Fagone, Enrico Finazzer, Arturo Giusti, Björn Huber, Andrea Lombardi, Aymeric Lopez, Marco Lucchetti, Gabriele Malavoglia, Luigi Manes, Giovanni Maressi, Francesco Mattesini, Daniele Notaro, Péter Mujzer, Federico Peirani, Alberto Peruffo, Maurizio Raggi, Andrea Alberto Tallillo, Antonio Tallillo, Roberto Vela, Massimo Zorza.

PUBLISHED BY
Luca Cristini Editore (Soldiershop), via Orio, 35/4 - 24050 Zanica (BG) ITALY.

DISTRIBUTION BY
Soldiershop - www.soldiershop.com, Amazon, Ingram Spark, Berliner Zinnfigurem (D), LaFeltrinelli, Mondadori, Libera Editorial (Spain), Google book (eBook), Kobo, (eBoook), Apple Book (eBook).

PUBLISHING'S NOTES
None of unpublished images or text of our book may be reproduced in any format without the expressed written permission of Luca Cristini Editore (already Soldiershop.com) when not indicate as marked with license creative commons 3.0 or 4.0. Luca Cristini Editore has made every reasonable effort to locate, contact and acknowledge rights holders and to correctly apply terms and conditions to Content. Every effort has been made to trace the copyright of all the photographs. If there are unintentional omissions, please contact the publisher in writing at: info@soldiershop.com, who will correct all subsequent editions.

LICENSES COMMONS
This book may utilize part of material marked with license creative commons 3.0 or 4.0 (CC BY 4.0), (CC BY-ND 4.0), (CC BY-SA 4.0) or (CC0 1.0). We give appropriate attribution credit and indicate if change were made in the acknowledgments field. Our WTW books series utilize only fonts licensed under the SIL Open Font License or other free use license.

CONTRIBUTORS OF THIS VOLUME & ACKNOWLEDGEMENTS
We would like to thank the main contributors to this issue: The profiles of the floats are all by the author. The colouring of the photos is by Anna Cristini. Special thanks to national and/or private institutions such as: Army General Staff, State Archives, Bundesarchiv, Nara, Library of Congress, Wikipedia, USAF, Signal magazine, War Chronicles, War Front, IWM, Australian War Museum, etc. A P.Crippa, A.Lopez, Péter Mujzer, L.Manes, C.Cucut, Tallillo archives. Model Victoria (www.modelvictoria.it) etc. for making available pictures or anything else from their archives. Special thanks to all modellers, their clubs and modelling companies for the courtesy use of their images. As far as possible we will always include the names of the authors. Please let us know in case you have not been able to locate them.

For a complete list of Soldiershop titles, or for every information please contact us on our website: www.soldiershop.com or www.cristinieditore.com. E-mail: info@soldiershop.com. Keep up to date on Facebook https://www.facebook.com/soldiershop.publishing

Title: **Light Tank Type 95 Ha-Go and derived** Code.: **TWE-037 EN**
Series by L. S. Cristini
ISBN code: 9791255892205 First edition March 2025
THE WEAPONS ENCYCLOPAEDIA (SOLDIERSHOP) is a trademark of Luca Cristini Editore

THE WEAPONS ENCYCLOPÆDIA
TANK AIRCRAFT AFV SHIP ARTILLERY VEHICLES SECRET WEAPON

LIGHT TANK TYPE 95 HA-GO AND DERIVED

LUCA STEFANO CRISTINI

BOOK SERIES FOR MODELERS & COLLECTORS

CONTENTS

Introduction .... pag. 5
   - Development .... pag. 7
   - Technical features of the vehicle .... pag. 13

Versions of the vehicle .... pag. 21
   - Other versions of the Ha-Go .... pag. 21
   - List of best-known Type 95 conversions .... pag. 22

Operational use .... pag. 33

Type 98 Ke-Ni .... pag. 53

Type 2 Ke-To .... pag. 55

Other users and export .... pag. 59

Camouflage and markings .... pag. 63

Type 95 Ha-Go - Modellism .... pag. 67

Data sheets .... pag. 16 Ha-Go, pag. 53 Ke-Ni, pag. 55 Ke-To

Bibliography .... pag. 70

▲ Japanese Type 95 Ha-Go light tank stored at the United States Army Ordnance Museum (Aberdeen) Courtesy of M Pellegrini CC1.

INTRODUCTION

The TType 95 Ha-Go was one of the most famous light tanks employed by Japan during World War II, used by both the armored regiments of the Imperial Army and the armored units of the Special Landing Forces of the Imperial Japanese Navy. Originally designed to support motorized infantry, it was able to move at the same speed as the troops and provide them with good tactical support. It was equipped with a 37 mm Type 94 gun and two 6.5 mm machine guns. It became Japan's main light tank, with about 2,000 produced until 1943 (sources, discordant, speak of production ranging from 1,100 to 2,300), including an improved version with a Type 98 37-mm cannon (at higher initial speed) and two Type 97 7.7-mm machine guns, which were more reliable than the earlier models.

The Type 95 was distinguished by its superiority in terms of speed and armament over most coeval vehicles of the mid-1930s. At the beginning of the Second Sino-Japanese War, it encountered no significant resistance, as the Chinese Nationalist forces had few armored vehicles and ineffective anti-tank weapons, and so it came out on top on that occasion. Between 1941 and 1942, the Type 95 still formed the backbone of the armored formations that participated in the conquest of Southeast Asia and the Philippines, operating even then often without encountering major obstacles. However, in the Philippines, a U.S.-controlled area, the tank's limitations began to emerge: armor that was immediately found to be very inadequate to deal with other armored vehicles (particularly the M3/M5 Stuart) and a main armament of inadequate power. Despite these critical issues, the Type 95 did not undergo significant improvements and remained virtually unchanged until the end of the war, continuing to be employed in the islands fortified by the Japanese and gradually conquered by the United States.

In these engagements, as a consequence, Japanese armored units were often annihilated. After Japan's surrender to the Allies, numerous Type 95s, which remained in China and Korea, fell into the hands of Nationalist and/or Communist forces.

▲ Japanese Type 95 Ha-Go light tank. One of the standard models with the flamboyant three-colour camouflage.

▲ Light Tank Type 95 Ha-Go profile as seen from above.

At home, the Type 95 served as the basis for the development of other light tanks, such as the Type 98 Ke-Ni and the Type 2 Ke-To, the latter of which could also be used by paratroopers. A major revision of the hull also led to the creation of the Type 2 Ka-Mi amphibious vehicle. However, all variants derived from the Type 95 were produced in limited numbers and only a few of them were sent to the front or tested in combat.

DEVELOPMENT

Following the creation in the early 1930s of mixed mechanized brigades within the Imperial Army it soon became apparent that the outdated Type 89 Yi-Go tanks were too slow and ill-suited to modern mobility needs. Therefore, a fast light vehicle with a long range and with weapons and armor comparable to foreign vehicles of the same category of the period was required, whose main task was the protection of the troops transported on the trucks.

The initial design phase of the new tank began in mid-1933, by Mitsubishi Heavy Industries in charge of development, and jointly at the Sagami and Kokura arsenals. By the summer of the following year, the prototype was completed at the Sagami arsenal. This was subjected to a series of tests, including 700 km endurance tests and firing evaluations. The vehicle received positive reviews, being praised for its excellent performance and good durability. The prototype reached a top speed of 43 km/h, could pass 2-meter wide trenches and had an operational range of 250 km.

However, the weight of the tank, which rose to 7.5 tons, was still considered too high. After some modifications, the weight was reduced to 6.5 tons. It is unclear how the excess ton was removed, but it is speculated that the thickness of the armor was decreased, along with a possible reduction in stored ammunition and changes to the suspension system. After these revisions, the tank underwent new tests, during which it reached a top speed of 45 km/h while also passing an endurance test over 370 km. In October 1934, the prototype was sent to the Cavalry School for further practical evaluations. The cavalry

▲ Production line of the Type 95 Ha-Go tank at the Mitsubishi factory.

▲ Light Tank Type 95 Ha-Go profile front and rear view.

TYPE 95 Ha-Go, JAPAN 1937

▲ Type 95 Ha-Go light tank with the first type of camouflage adopted in the late 1930s. Japan 1937.

TYPE 95 Ha-Go, JAPAN 1938-1940

▲ Type 95 Ha-Go light tank in the basic variant, painted in Quantung Army camouflage, commonly used in the late 1930s and early 1940s.

expressed great satisfaction, considering the vehicle a light, mobile and maneuverable tank that was ideal for their needs. In contrast, the infantry was not as enthusiastic, criticizing the modest 37-mm gun as inadequate and the 12-mm armored protection as insufficient.

This disagreement between the two branches of the Japanese armed forces led to a further period of testing in late 1934 and early 1935, conducted this time in northern Manchuria during the winter season. The tests were supervised by an independent Mixed Brigade consisting of infantry and cavalry stationed in the region. The final report was positive, and indicated that the tank was ready for service, demonstrating good performance even in harsh weather conditions. The Mixed Brigade then requested to be equipped with the new tank as soon as possible, to replace the old Type 92 Jyu-Sokosha armored cars already in use. The new tank, already designed in 1935, began to be produced and distributed in limited quantities from the following year. However, it was not until 1938 that production accelerated, peaking in 1941 with as many as 705 units produced. Production finally ended in 1943. The total number of units built, however, remains uncertain, with estimates varying widely among sources: some indicate between 1,100 and 1,250 units while the most generous speak of as many as 2,375.

Mitsubishi, as mentioned above was the main company responsible for production, flanked by the Sagami and Kokura arsenals operated by the Army. Other companies that contributed to the tank's production were Hitachi, Niigata Tekkosho and Kōbe Seikosho. After the tank was accepted, it was named the Type 95 Ha-Go (Japanese: kyūgo-shiki kei-sensha Ha-Gō). The number 95 was given after the Japanese

▶ An early production Type 95; later the shape of the pilot's visor, side hull and wheels changed.

▲ Another good image of a 95 Ha-Go tank preserved in excellent condition.

● LIGHT TANK TYPE 95 HA-GO AND DERIVATIVES

TYPE 95 Ha-Go, JAPAN 1939

▲ Type 95 Ha-Go light tank. Kwantung Army in 1939.

LIGHT TANK TYPE 95 HA-GO AND DERIVATIVES

imperial year (otherwise known as Kōki) 2595 (equal to western 1935). Ha-Go, on the other hand, stands for "third model," but is also known as "Ke-go," which can be translated as the third light vehicle. In some sources, it is also marked as Kyu-Go.

TECHNICAL CHARACTERISTICS OF THE VEHICLE

The tank's **hull** was modernly lined internally with asbestos to protect the three-man crew from the intense heat of tropical climates. The pilot occupied the driver's seat on the right, and was able to take advantage of a visor and slit cut out on a hatch that was usually left open when not in combat, again for "thermal" reasons. To his left, slightly ahead, was the operator of the 6.5 mm Type 91 machine gun, mounted on a ball mount with a 35° arc of fire on either side. In addition to operating the machine gun, the operator was responsible for operating the engine and using the radio, when present, since the latter was not standard equipment on Japanese tanks. The commander, the sole occupant of the "small" off-center turret on the left, had the task of operating the main armament consisting of the gun, giving orders to the driver and coordinating with other units, a workload certainly too onerous for one person. The driver in turn was positioned at the right front of the tank. He guided the vehicle by the traditional method, that is, using two rudders.

The driver's hatch was rounded and bonnet-like, positioned at the front. The driver could see out the hatch in three ways. For maximum protection, the hatch would be closed, but there were three simple, narrow slits cut out for limited vision. Unusually for the time, the vision slots were modernly protected by reinforced glass that was placed in rubber mounts inside the hatch. For a slightly better but still protected view, there was a smaller square hatch in the center of the hood. When the tank was not engaged in combat, partly because of the heat, as repeatedly mentioned, the hood could, of course, be fully open while driving.

▲ Nice picture of two Type 95 Ha-Go operating in a typical tropical environment. Note the Japanese flags painted on the front of the vehicle.

The **armament** and **turret**. The latter, rotatable manually on a 90° frontal arc, housed the main weapon: a Type 94 37-mm cannon (designated L/36.7) with an initial speed of 583 m/s, capable of piercing a 45-mm plate at a range of 300 meters. The cannon, slightly off-center to the right, could rise from -15° to +20° and rotate independently of the turret over an arc of 20°. Completing the armament for the busy tank commander was also a second Type 91 6.5 mm machine gun (in addition to the servant gun), also positioned in the turret but 120° to the right. However, this configuration, designed to provide the commander with two weapons with minimal turret rotation, proved ineffective in practice. The large amount of ammunition carried (over 110 rounds for the gun and nearly 3,000 rounds for the two machine guns) created stowage problems, and consequently made the space for the three-man crew even tighter. This resulted in truly poor tank habitability, with the crew confined to cramped quarters. In tropical theaters of operation, the pilot often left visors and hatches open even during combat.

In the late 1930s and early 1940s, it was decided to replace the old 37-mm cannon with a Type 98 of the same caliber but with a larger firing chamber, which increased the initial speed to 685 m/s, allowing a 25-mm plate to be pierced even at 500 meters. The machine guns were also upgraded, replaced with two 7.7 mm Type 97s. The weight of the tank thus returned to the original 7.4 tons that gave so much thought to the tank's engineers at its inception.

At the rear of the square-shaped hull were housed: the engine, tanks, and air cooling system. On the outer right side were the exhaust and muffler, while three hatches (an upper one with a ventilation grille) provided access for maintenance. The tank's engine initially was a 118-hp Daimler, already used on the medium Type 89 Yi-Go tank, but it was soon replaced with a more advanced 120-hp 6-cylinder Mitsubishi NVD 6120, which offered higher speed and a fuel consumption of 66 liters per 100 km. The electric ignition system ran on 24 volts, and the manual transmission had four forward gears and one reverse gear. The front transmission required the addition of two nose hatches to facilitate maintenance operations.

◀▼ Two more pictures of the tank on page 11 allow you to see the particular shape of the turret, especially the one seen from above.

The Type 95 used the same **rolling train** as the older Japanese Type 94 TK tankettes, featuring a front drive wheel with double sprocket and a rear idler wheel, which also adjusted track tension. These, 251 mm wide, were composed of 98 elements with a central tooth guide, providing a ground pressure of 0.61 kg/cm². The four load-bearing wheels, coupled in two bogies, were connected to longitudinal swing arms, anchored to a large coil spring mounted parallel to the ground and protected by a steel sheath attached to the side of the hull. Completing the rolling train were two double idler rollers. This suspension system, typical of Japanese tanks, converted vertical movements into horizontal ones, which were

▲ Picture of the prototype taken from an original manual with the parts of the vehicle indicated in Japanese.

TYPE 95 Ha-Go DATA SHEET	
Dimensions	4.38 length x 2.07 width x 2.28 height (in m)
Weight	7,4 t
Crew	3 (commander/cannoneer, driver and gunner/mechanic)
Entry and withdrawal from service	December 1936-1943
Fuel capacity	164 litres
Engine	Mitsubishi diesel NVD 6120 6-cylinder, air-cooled
Maximum speed	45 km/h on road, 32 km/h off road
Autonomy	250 km, 170 km off road
Power	120 CV
Armament	1 cannon 37mm Type 97
Secondary armament	2 Type 97 7.7 mm Arisaka machine guns
Armour	9-12 mm front, 12 mm side, 6-12 mm rear
Production	About 1161 (according to others sources 2300)
Users	Japanese Empire, Thailand, China

▲ From top left: detail of the visors available to the tank driver/pilot. Right: the curious contraption on the back of the tank to enable the infantry to communicate with the tank commander from the outside. Below: one of the two Manchu suspensions placed on each side/side of the Type 95 tracks.

then absorbed by the spring. However, during testing, a problem emerged: the distance between the load-bearing wheels coincided with that of the furrows in the plowed ground chosen for testing. To solve the problem, the bogies were turned upside down and fitted with additional small wheels on the pivots. The Type 95's **armor**, made of riveted plates, had an average thickness of 12 mm on the hull sides and nose, with a modest slope. The turret, with the same thickness on all sides, was protected by a 57 mm thick mantle. These protections, although sufficient to repel all light 7.7 mm shells, were considered adequate only for the Chinese theater of operations, where antitank weapons were rare and Japanese tanks could operate and run with relative freedom. However, the vulnerability of these armors became evident during the Battle of Khalkhin Gol against the Soviets and against all American armored units. Finally, the Type 95 could overcome trenches up to 2.01 meters wide, vertical obstacles 0.73 meters high and fords 1.03 meters deep.

One feature we have already mentioned that was very innovative about the Type 95 was that the interior surfaces were covered with layers of asbestos. This had two purposes, in addition to the one already mentioned due to

▶ Detail of one of the two 7.7 mm Type 97 heavy machine guns. Note the top-loading magazine, and the structure of the shield.

▲ An Australian soldier studying the disassembled Type 95 gun with its accompanying 37 mm ammunition stockpile. Author's colouring.

● LIGHT TANK TYPE 95 HA-GO AND DERIVATIVES

the extreme heat of tropical climates, asbestos insulation had the added benefit of providing some padding to the interior surfaces, giving the crew a little more comfort over rough terrain. However, the very serious health problems caused by asbestos were not widely known at the time.

The **radio** was the preserve of the command tank only. Everyone else had to make do with signal flags to communicate with other vehicles. Vehicles equipped with radios could be easily distinguished by the round Russian-type antenna mounted on top of the turret.

Finally, a unique feature that distinguished the original infantry support role of the Type 95 was a kind of microphone for infantry use placed externally on the rear of the vehicle. This was a very curious feature of the Type 95 indeed. This microphone was camouflaged by a shape resembling a mock bolt head. Infantry outside the tank used it to hold communications with the tank commander. The Type 95 was one of the first, few tanks ever to have such a feature.

▲ From top left: nice picture of a Japanese tank commander. Right: a Type 95 Ha-Go tank engaged in a series of vehicle evaluation tests. Below right: a Type 95 knocked out by US marines at Garapan on the island of Saipan in June 1944. Author's colours.

TYPE 95 Ha-Go, JAPAN 1940

▲ Type 95 Ha-Go light tank, command tank version with antenna and typical 'Manchu' sops mounted in reverse. Chinese front. Japanese Army 1940.

LIGHT TANK TYPE 95 HA-GO AND DERIVATIVES

TYPE 95 Ha-Go, JAPAN 1941

▲ Type 95 Ha-Go light tank. Basic variant of the vehicle for use by the Special Landing Forces of the Japanese Navy, 1941.

VERSIONS OF THE VEHICLE

■ THE OTHER VERSIONS OF THE HA-GO

As with many other iconic tanks, the Type 95 served as a starting point for the creation of a good number of variables of more advanced and better equipped light tanks, as well as all-purpose vehicles. However, Japan's war industry, already worn out by years of war and heavily engaged in shipbuilding and repair, and with difficulties in sourcing raw material managed to produce only a few hundred of these new vehicles, many of which even remained at the prototype stage. An early attempt was the Type 3 Ke-Ri, which integrated a 57-mm gun from the Type 97 Chi-Ha, but the defective turret design and difficulties in using the weapon limited its success. This model was soon replaced by the Type 4 Ke-Nu, which directly adopted the Type 97 turret with the same armament.

Later, the Type 2 Ka-Mi amphibious tank, equipped with floating structures and two external propeller engines for navigation, was also developed. A design dating back to the late 1930s led instead to the Type 98 Ke-Ni, produced in fewer than 100 examples because it was considered only marginally superior to the Type 95 and thus ineffective against Allied tanks. In 1945 the Type 5 Ho-Ru was designed, a light tank fighter that, however, never saw combat use.

A training version of the Type 95 was also made, called the Manshū, equipped with small additional wheels between the tracks, but also usable in battle. During the conflict, attempts were made to turn it into an anti-aircraft self-propelled vehicle, the Ta-Se, by equipping it with a 20-mm cannon, but the design remained experimental. Instead, the Type 95 Ri-Ki, equipped with a 3-ton crane, was created for the engineers.

Another experimental model, the Ho-To, sacrificed the turret to accommodate a 120-mm mortar in a casemate, but this too had no further development.

▲ The Type 2 Ka-Mi amphibious tank derived, with various modifications, from the Type 95. Author's colouring.

LIST OF THE MOST WELL-KNOWN TYPE 95 CONVERSIONS

• Type 95 Ha-Go (first production)

An early production version (see photo on p. 11) that differed from the final and most-produced model in adopting less powerful armament: the main gun was a 37 mm Type 94 with a barrel length of 36.7 calibers, muzzle velocity of 575 (1900 fps) 600 m/s (2200 fps) and armor penetration of 45 mm at 300 m (1.48 inches at 300 yards). Secondary armament, however, consisted of two Type 91 6.5 mm machine guns. Produced until 1937 in less than 100 examples. It was used in Manchuku and China. Of this variant, the first production tanks used the old 110-hp (82 kW) Mitsubishi engine (like that used in the Type 89 I-Go medium tank) and had a top speed of 25 mph (40 km/h).

• Type 95 Ha-Go (Hokuman or Manshû version)

Due to problems encountered in Manchukuò with sorghum grass in the fields getting trapped in the suspension/wheels, the wheel and suspension components were reversed with the addition of small wheels mounted on the square crank axle so that the tanks could move freely in the grass. This modified version was used in the Battle of Nomohan. Sometimes this type of tank was informally called the "Manchurian model" or Type 95 Manshû. It was mainly used as a training tank (and only later became operational as well) and equipped the instruction unit of the Kwantung Military Academy in Manchukuò.

• Type 95 Ha-Go (late production)

Among other improvements to the engine and main gun, the secondary armament was changed to two Type 97 7.7 mm machine guns, one in the rear section of the turret and one in the front hull.

• Ri-Ki crane vehicle type 95

The Type 95 Ri-Ki was a tracked vehicle created for the Army Corps of Engineers. At the rear of the chassis, it had a 3-ton, 4.5-meter "boom crane." Also made later on the hull of the Type Ke-Ni and/or Ke-To.

▲ The Type 95 tank boasted a very modern asymmetric track suspension system. Author's colouring.

TYPE 95 Ha-Go, PHILIPPINES 1942

▲ Type 95 Ha-Go light tank of the 7th Japan Army Tank Regiment at Luzon in the Philippines, 1942.

TYPE 95 Ha-Go, JAPAN 1944

▲ Type 95 Ha-Go light tank of the 9th Armoured Regiment of the Imperial Army. This tank once again features the typical camouflage of the imperial navy from which it came. June 1944, Saipan.

- **Type 95 Ta-Se**

Anti-aircraft tank designed in November 1941. Armed with a 20-mm cannon.

- **So-Ki type 95 armored railway carriage**

The Type 95 So-Ki was an armored rail car designed at the request of the Kwantung Army to patrol and guard remote narrow-gauge railway lines. The vehicle was equipped with a retractable wheel system underneath to enable it to travel on the tracks. Between 121 and 138 units were produced between 1935 and 1943 and operated in both China and Burma.

- **Ka-Mi type 2 amphibious tank**

This was the first amphibious tank produced in Japan and was intended for use by the Japanese Naval Special Landing Forces. The chassis was based on the Type 95 Ha-Go and its main armament was the same, a 37 mm tank gun. The two pontoons (front-to-back) were attached by a system of "small clips" with a release inside the tank, to be engaged once it landed for ground combat operations. The Type 2 Ka-Mi was first used in combat at Guadalcanal in late 1942. They were later encountered by the U.S. Marine Corps in the Marshall Islands and the Mariana Islands, particularly on Saipan. They were also used during fighting on the Philippine island of Leyte in late 1944. They were produced from 1942 to 1944, in about 182-184 completed units.

- **Ke-Ri Prototype Type 3**

This was a proposed model with a Type 97 57 mm tank gun as the main armament in a modified turret. The chassis was the same as the Type 95 Ha-Go. The light tank had a weight of 7.4 tons and a crew of 3 men. However, a significant dis-

▲ Type 2 Ka-Mi amphibious tanks without their flotation sections, photographed after capture by Australian soldiers, Pacific Front 1945. Pictured here is a small image of the army engineer version with a crane installed. It was made with both the 95 chassis and the Ke-Ni version, as in this case.

advantage was identified: despite the adoption of the new, heavier 5.7-cm gun, the reuse of the Type 95 Ha-Go tank turret made the usable space inside the tank even more cramped, making it arduous and challenging to operate the weapon. A small number of prototypes were produced, however, the design never made it past the test-testing phase carried out in the field in 1943.

- **Ho-To Prototype Type 4**

The Ho-To was a self-propelled gun on a modified Ha-Go chassis. It mounted a 120-mm Type 38 howitzer in an open casemate with front and side armor. A prototype was completed. However, this howitzer had a rather low muzzle velocity, but nevertheless, its high-explosive projectiles could destroy a Sherman.

- **Ho-Ru Prototype Type 5**

The Ho-Ru was a light tank fighter similar to the German Hetzer , but armed with the weaker 47 mm main gun in a semi-enclosed casemate. The Type 5 Ho-Ru used the chassis of the Type 95 Ha-Go, the suspension was widened to accommodate 350 mm wide tracks with double center rails. There were two rows of wheel guide pins, which held a road wheel between them. The drive wheel sprocket was of the grid type to engage with the wheel guide pins as on the Soviet T-34. Development of the Type 5 Ho-Ru began in February 1945 with only one prototype completed before the end of the war.

- **Type 98 Ke-Ni**

The Type 98 Ke-Ni was a light tank designed by the Japanese Empire in the late 1930s as a replacement for the Type 95 Ha-Go, but put into production only during World War II, starting in 1942.

Armed with a 37-mm cannon and a 7.7-mm machine gun, it did not represent a marked improvement on the Type 95 and therefore manufacture was modest with just over a hundred examples.

▲ Type 4 Ho-To SPG self-propelled tank with 12 cm Type 38 howitzer. In the small picture: two Ke-Ri Type 3 tanks during operational tests to which they were subjected and which did not give a favourable opinion.

TYPE 95 Ha-Go, JAPAN 1944

▲ Type 95 Ha-Go Light Tank Company, 14th Infantry Division, Imperial Army - September 1944, Peleliu.

TYPE 95 Ha-Go, JAPAN 1944

▲ Type 95 Ha-Go light tank of the Army of Japan engaged in the Saipan (Mariana Islands) campaign, summer 1944.

- **Ke-To type 2**

The Type 2 Ke-To was a light tank developed in Japan during World War II, a direct evolution of the armored Type 98 Ke-Ni and a candidate to replace both this and the now outdated Type 95 Ha-Go: however, the difficult situation of the Japanese Empire during the war meant that very few vehicles were produced.

- **Ke-Nu conversion type 4**

A conversion that replaced the existing Type 95 Ha-Go turret with the larger Type 97 Chi-Ha turret usable by two men, armed with the 57 mm low-velocity tank gun. The conversions were carried out toward the end of the war, with an estimate indicating about 100 units made before the end of the conflict.

▲ Ke-Nu Type light assault tank preserved at the Victory Park in Moscow. Above in the two small photos: two views of the Ka-Mi amphibious vehicle preserved in a museum and a ruin left to rust in the jungle.

TYPE 95 Ha-Go, JAPAN 1945

▲ Type 95 Ha-Go light tank belonging to the 79th Infantry Division, Kwantung Army, China and Manchukuò, August 1945.

▲ Still a Ka-Mi amphibian preserved in an open-air museum.

▲ A Ha-Go was discovered in 2015 on the island of Shumshu in the Kurili archipelago. Brought and restored in Russia, it is now on display in the Kubinka Museum in Moscow.

LIGHT TANK TYPE 95 HA-GO AND DERIVATIVES

TYPE 95 Ha-Go, CHINA 1945

▲ Type 95 Ha-Go light tank captured by communist guerrillas in China, where it remained in use years after the war. It wore the five-pointed star on an all-green camouflage of the Chinese Red Forces.

OPERATIONAL USE

The Type 95 was made available to cavalry units and brigades attached to infantry formations to replace their old Type 92. The autonomous mixed brigade made use of this tank during the first offensives of the 1937 China campaign. Facing almost no anti-tank opposition, this tank could not demonstrate its real potential. However, at that time, infantry distrust of this tank dissipated and the Type 95 was also employed in tank regiments; a company of 10 tanks (3 platoons of 3 tanks + 1 command tank), while some were employed in the command company.

■ THE CAMPAIGN IN CHINA AND MONGOLIA 1937

After the start of the Second Sino-Japanese War, the Imperial Japanese Army mobilized an independent armored brigade, led by Major General Sakai, consisting of twelve Type 89 Yi-Go tanks, twelve Type 94 TK tanks, four armored engineer vehicles, and thirteen Type 95 tanks making their first appearance in a conflict. After fighting in the Beijing and Hebei areas, the armored brigade reached Quhar province, where it was divided among infantry units to support its advance.

However, the lack of anti-tank weapons and armored vehicles on the Chinese side made the task of the Type 95 light tanks relatively easy. However, the inadequate performance of this unit led to the disbandment of the Mixed Mechanized Brigade. After this, the tank units would be used mainly as support elements of the infantry divisions.

▲ Japanese Ha-Go tanks examined by Russian troops after their capture following the Battle of Khalkin God in Quantung at the end of the war.

Although the war with China continued for another few years until 1945, the use of Type 95s took a back seat, Reported their presence in Manchuria and northern China, most were moved and reused on the Pacific front until the end of the war.

About two years later, in the summer of 1939, Japan and the Soviet Union clashed in yet another undeclared border war at Nomonhan, ending a series of similar conflicts that had begun in the early 1930s. The Japanese sent two tank regiments, including the 4th Regiment thirty-six Type 95 tanks strong. This clash, known as the Battle of Khalkin God was the true war baptism of the Ha-Go tank! During the first armored clash, the Japanese vehicles proved inadequate due to their poor protection and short-barreled guns. In only ten days of battle, they lost more than 40 percent of their manpower. The Russian vehicles were certainly not what China had.

The simultaneous signing of the Molotov-Ribbentrop Pact (between Germany and the Soviet Union) eventually forced the Japanese to call it quits and turn their attention to the Pacific and Southeast Asia.

■ MALAYSIA, BURMA, AND THE FIRST CLASHES WITH THE ALLIES 1941-1942

Following Japanese military operations in Asia, particularly the occupation of French Indochina, the United States, along with Canada and Britain, imposed economic sanctions on Japan.

Among these, the oil embargo had a particularly severe impact, as Japan was heavily dependent on crude oil imports. This move by the Allies, combined with other pressures, helped push Japan toward open and total conflict. Initially, the Allies underestimated the threat, believing that Japan lacked the resources to launch simultaneous attacks on multiple fronts. However, war with the United States officially broke out after the attack on Pearl Harbor in December 1941. At the same time, the Japanese sought to weaken the British navy in the Pacific by initiating a series of large-scale offensives. Meanwhile, the Type 95 tank was by this time a six-year-old tank, already considered obsolete compared to other nations' armored vehicles, especially when compared with European vehicles. However, it was successfully used during Japan's rapid expansion into the Pacific.

▲ Australian 2 pdr anti-tank gun in action at Bakri a Malaysia against a Ha-Go Type 95.

▲ A Ha-Go Type 95 tank whose turret was decapitated, analysed by US marines.

Japan's main goal was the conquest of Malaya and the Philippines.

Japanese troops landed in Malaya on December 8, 1941, supported by three armored units: the 1st Tank Regiment (commanded by Colonel Mukaida), the 6th Regiment (commanded by Colonel Kawamura) and the 14th Regiment (commanded by Colonel Kita).

During the invasion, which began in December 1941, the three Japanese armored regiments consisted mainly of 40 Type 97 Chi-Ha tanks and 12 Type 95 Ha-Go tanks each, totaling about 211 vehicles. The British, who were defending the region, did not expect massive use of armored vehicles due to the impassable terrain and scarcity of suitable roads. However, the Japanese tanks demonstrated remarkable mobility, advancing effectively despite the difficult terrain, thanks in part to the support of infantry and bicycle units.

The Type 95 and Type 97 proved decisive in clashes against Indian troops defending the Alor Setar air base. The speed and aggressiveness of the Japanese tanks caused panic among the Indian ranks, forcing them into a disorderly retreat. Next, the Japanese attacked the Allied defensive line at Jitra, where the combination of tanks and cycling units again caused chaos, collapsing the enemy defenses and forcing some units to flee.

In all operations the Type 95 light tanks advanced smoothly, demonstrating the special vocation for which they were designed, contributing to the conquest of the Malay Peninsula and the landing in Singapore on Feb. 8, where they were instrumental in overcoming British resistance.

In Burma, however, the situation was different. The British deployed the 7th Armored Brigade against the 1st Company of the Japanese 2nd Tank Regiment, which had only twelve Type 95s under the command of Lieutenant Okada. The Japanese vehicles suffered several defeats against the M3 Stuart light tanks, which nevertheless remained vulnerable to infantry attacks. Eventually, the Indo-British troops were still forced to withdraw from Burma. In total, the Japanese fielded about 400 tanks for these missions. For these early operations, it should be noted that the Allies had a limited number of armored vehicles at the end of 1941. British and Dutch forces were equipped mainly with obsolete light tanks and armored cars, as well as a small contingent of M3A1 tanks. The United States, on the other hand, deployed the 192nd and 194th Tank Battalions, with 108 M3 tanks and fifty 75mm self-propelled guns.

TYPE 95 Ha-Go, THAILAND 1945

▲ Type 95 Ha-Go light tank ceded to the Thai army allied with the Japanese and renamed Type 83 by them. Thailand, 1945.

THE CONQUEST OF SINGAPORE

In early January, Japanese troops approached the last defensive lines before Singapore. Although the first assault had been repulsed, Japanese soldiers discovered an abandoned and unguarded road leading directly to Allied positions. Taking advantage of this opportunity, tanks and infantry moved quickly to encircle the enemy forces. By late January, after covering about 900 kilometers, the Japanese reached the suburbs of Singapore.

Allied forces in Singapore amounted to as many as 70,000 men, while the Japanese could count on only 30,000 soldiers. Despite the large disparity in numbers, after intense fighting, the Allies were forced to surrender on February 15, 1942. In this operation, Japanese tanks, particularly the Type 95, played a crucial role. Although their 37 mm cannon proved ineffective against bunkers or fortifications, their mobility and ease of repair made them a powerful psychological weapon. Allied soldiers, convinced that tanks could not be effectively employed in that theater, were taken by surprise by the agility and determination of the Japanese armored forces.

PHILIPPINES, DUTCH INDIES, ALEUTIAN ISLANDS, AND OTHER ARCHIPELAGOS AND ISLANDS

Before 1941, Japan, realizing the superiority of many Allied armored vehicles, undertook a series of initiatives aimed at upgrading its armored arsenal, improving vehicle performance, and restructuring the organization of dedicated units. Although some goals, such as increasing the number of tanks and developing more effective armaments, were partially achieved, a significant expansion in the production and distribution of armored vehicles, as well as the development of more advanced models, proved impractical. The reasons lay in the country's limited industrial capabilities and the priority given to other

▲ One of the Type 95s sent to Leyte leaves the transport ship that brought it to the island.

▲▼ A Type 95 on display at the Australian War Memorial. Below: the same being restored.

branches of the armed forces, such as the Navy and Air Force.

Despite these difficulties, the Japanese Army managed to establish several new armored regiments and equip at least 10 infantry divisions with organic companies of tanks, each equipped with 9 Type 95 vehicles. At the outbreak of operations in the Southwest Pacific, Japan had about 2,200 tanks, with the Type 95 making up the majority of the available fleet.

Meanwhile came the turn of the Philippines, under U.S. control since 1898, which was attacked soon after Pearl Harbor by the Japanese 14th Army. The beginning of the battle for the Philippines dates back to the night of December 8-9, 1941. For this operation, the Japanese deployed about 160 tanks, including several Type 95s. Facing them, the American armored forces were represented mainly by the 192nd and 194th Tank Battalions. During the amphibious landings near Lingayen, the Japanese employed about 100 tanks, using special transport ships equipped with bow ramps, which allowed the vehicles to land quickly and engage the enemy immediately.

On December 22, Japanese Type 95 tanks clashed with a group of five American M3 tanks near Damortis. In a brief clash, one M3 was destroyed, while the others retreated. However, on December 31, the Americans took revenge by destroying eight Type 95s. In early January 1942, Japanese forces, supported by tanks and infantry, succeeded in capturing Manila. The Americans, in response, retreated to Bataan, fortifying the position with their two armored battalions.

The Japanese 65th Infantry Division, supported by about 50 tanks, was tasked with breaking through the American defenses. However, the Japanese tanks encountered difficulties as their guns proved less effective against the M3s, suffering several casualties. The Americans, on the other hand, employed the M3s in small units, effectively making them vulnerable to concentrated anti-tank fire from the Japanese. Despite

▶▼ Japanese Ha-Go tanks examined by Russian troops after their capture in Quantung at the end of the war.

Below: a Japanese tank driver is photographed in front of his Ha-Go tank.

LIGHT TANK TYPE 95 HA-GO AND DERIVATIVES

TYPE 95 Ha-Go, FRANCE-INDOCHINA 1950-53

▲ Type 95 Ha-Go 'Joffre' light tank captured and converted by French forces present in Indochina in the early 1950s.

numerous tank-supported attacks, the Japanese initially failed to penetrate enemy lines.

To reinforce the offensive, the Japanese sent 45,000 new soldiers, while the 4th Armored Regiment was withdrawn for use in other campaigns. Exactly was sent west to successfully participate in the conquest of the Dutch East Indies. The American defenses finally collapsed in early April. During the retreat, the M3s supported the American infantry in skirmishes against the Japanese 7th Armored Regiment. In these fights, the two American tank battalions were annihilated, and some of their vehicles even ended up captured by the Japanese.

The Dutch East Indies, at the time were territories, controlled by the Netherlands, and were a strategic target for Japan because of their rich oil fields. In addition to the 4th Regiment diverted from the Philippine theater, the 2nd Tank Regiment (commanded by Colonel Mori) was also deployed, consisting of thirty-one Type 97 Chi-Ha medium tanks and six Type 95s. These vehicles operated successfully, easily overcoming weak Allied resistance.

Finally, as the air-sea battle of Midway drew to a close, Japanese troops landed on June 10, 1942, on the two westernmost islands of the Aleutians, Attu and Kiska, conquering both.

Also among the invading Japanese forces were some Type 95 tanks, which thus became the only armored vehicles of an enemy nation to tread on U.S. soil in wartime. However, there are no further significant details about their fate after the landing.

■ U.S. COUNTEROFFENSIVE BEGINS

In July 1942, the strategic initiative passed to the United States after victories at the Battle of the Coral Sea and Midway. In August, the Americans attacked Guadalcanal, while in New Guinea Allied troops held out tenaciously at Port Moresby. To counter the Australian-U.S. forces, the Japanese devised a plan involving a land advance and landing in Milne Bay. In late August, divisions of the 5th Landing Force "Kure" landed unopposed, supported by a platoon of two Type 95s. However, the tanks bogged down despite their low weight and were abandoned, with no participation in the battle.

▲ A Type 95 light tank on public display in a square in Manila, the capital of the Philippines.

▲▶ Two Marine soldiers observe a captured Japanese tank on the island of Guam.

Right: a Type 95 knocked out during the Battle of Tarawa.

The Australians managed to push back the Japanese troops after several days of fighting.

At Guadalcanal in October 1942, the independent 1st Tank Company arrived, consisting of ten Type 97 Chi-Ha medium tanks and two Type 95s. This unit, under the command of Captain Maeda, had been created by converting the 4th Company of the 2nd Regiment after the conquest of the Dutch Indies. During the landing, two Type 97s were damaged, but the other vehicles advanced with the 4th Infantry Regiment toward the Matanikau River, west of the American positions defending Henderson Airport. An initial attack was launched on the evening of October 21, but the leading Type 95 was destroyed by 155 mm howitzer fire, forcing the Japanese to retreat. The offensive resumed on October 23, with the tanks paving the way for the 4th Regiment. However, the lead tank was hit by an anti-tank gun and destroyed, quickly followed by the other vehicles, all of which were eliminated.

After the loss of Guadalcanal and with the strategic initiative now in U.S. hands, the Type 95 had become obsolete compared to mass-produced American armor and weapons. It proved vulnerable even to Browning M2 12.7 mm heavy machine guns. Armor-piercing shells often passed through its thin armor without exploding, forcing Allied crews to use explosive grenades, which proved more than sufficient to neutralize it.

In Tarawa Atoll on Betio Island, the Japanese had built fortifications and deployed an armored unit of the 7th Special Landing Force, consisting of fourteen Type 95s under the command of Ensign Ohtani. During the battle, seven Japanese tanks attacked an American M4 Sherman, but were quickly overwhelmed and destroyed. On Makin Island, a detachment of the 3rd Special Base Force was supported by three Type 95s: one was destroyed in combat, while the other two were abandoned in a fortified position.

Between January and February 1944, the United States launched the Marshall campaign, attacking with massive preliminary bombardment. On Eniwetok Island, the Marines clashed with the tank company of the 1st Mobile Marine Brigade, consisting of nine Type 95s under the command of First Lieutenant Ichikawa, who, however, was not present during the clash. The unit was completely destroyed. On Parry Island in the southeastern part of Eniwetok Atoll, three more Type 95s were eliminated during and after the February 22 landings.

OPERATIONS IN NEW GUINEA, INDIA AND CHINA

Japanese troops in New Guinea, already weakened by the Allied offensive in the summer of 1943, maintained control of the western part of the island. However, they were subjected to intense air attacks by Task Force 58, which set the stage for the Allied landings on April 22, 1944. Isolated, the Nipponese units faced a further U.S. landing on May 27 on Biak Island, where 11,000 Imperial soldiers supported by tanks from the 222nd Infantry Regiment were deployed. Despite counterattacks led by Lt. Iwasa, the Japanese gradually lost ground, culminating in the fall of Biak airfield on June 15.

At the same time, other Allied landings in New Guinea led to clashes such as Toem, where the U.S. 7th Amphibious Force clashed with the Japanese 36th Infantry Division, supported by Type 95 tanks. Despite some initial successes, such as the destruction of a U.S. amphibious tank on July 3, the Japanese were forced to withdraw, leaving Sarmi isolated and without strategic value.

In India and China, however, military operations had stalled since the summer of 1942. The Japanese concentrated their efforts in the Pacific for a long time, while the Chinese and British had to use equal time to prepare a major offensive. However, in March 1944, the Japanese anticipated everyone, launching an attack toward India from Burma, involving the 14th Tank Regiment.

Despite the use of numerous armored vehicles, the operation ended in serious defeat, especially at the Battle of Kohima, where the regiment was almost completely destroyed.

▲ Type 95 Ha-Go tanks of the 16th Armoured Regiment on Marcus Island (Minami Torishima), 1942-43.

Ke-Ri PROTOTYPE, JAPAN 1943

▲ Prototype of the Ke-Ri armed with a 57 mm Type 97 gun in a new turret. Test phase never passed. 1943.

In China, the Japanese launched Operation Ichi-Go in April 1944, achieving significant successes such as capturing Luoyang, Changsha and Liuzhou. By December, Japanese troops reached Indochina, establishing a continuous rail link from Manchuria to Southeast Asia.

WAR IN THE MARIANA ISLANDS

In the Marianas, a Japanese possession since 1919, the Allies began landings on June 15, 1944, on Saipan Island. The Japanese, with the 9th Tank Regiment and other armored units, launched a series of counterattacks, including a massive night charge on June 17. However, the Americans, supported by Sherman tanks and artillery, repelled the assaults, destroying most of the Nipponese vehicles.

On Guam, the Marines landed on July 21, facing Japanese tanks in a series of engagements that led to the destruction of most of the Type 95s. On Tinian, the last island in the Marianas to be invaded, the Japanese also attempted counterattacks with their tanks, but were quickly neutralized.

Finally, at Peleliu, the Japanese, with 16 Type 95s, launched a counterattack on September 15, 1944, but were repulsed by Marines supported by Sherman tanks. The battle ended with the destruction of the Japanese armored unit and the Allied victory.

Operations in New Guinea, India, China and the Marianas highlighted the growing Allied superiority in terms of armor and strategy. Despite valiant Japanese counterattacks, lack of resources and Allied firepower led to a series of defeats that marked the decline of Japanese expansion in the Pacific.

▶ A Type 95 tank destroyed during the Battle of Tinian Island in the Marianas.

▲ Despite the extreme courage shown by the Japanese soldiers, the superiority of the Allied forces became increasingly apparent towards the end of the war, resulting in the destruction of most of the Japanese armoured forces. Courtesy by Australian war memorial.

Ri-Ki CRANE VEHICLE TYPE 95/98/2, JAPAN 1944

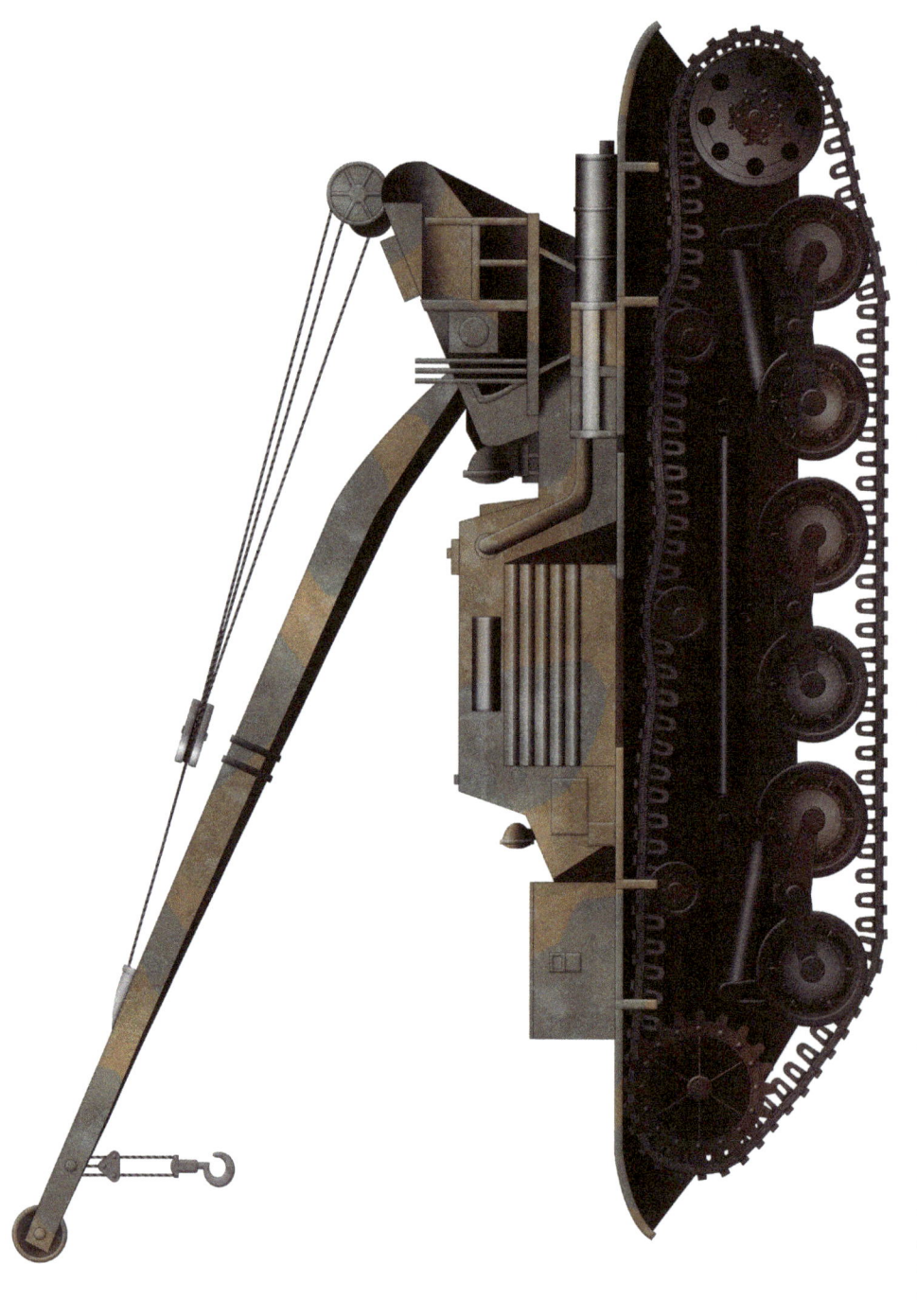

▲ Vehicle for the Army Corps of Engineers that was derived from the Type 95 Ha-Go, the Type 98 Ke-Ni and the Type 2 Ke-To referred to in the profile.

LIBERATION OF THE PHILIPPINES

After consolidating control over Peleliu and New Guinea, the United States turned its attention to the Philippines, a crucial strategic oil supply point from Japan. Intense aerial bombardment preceded the landing on Leyte Island on October 20, 1944. The Japanese, with only one armored unit equipped with obsolete Type 89 Yi-Go tanks, attempted to repel the invaders, but suffered heavy losses.

Determined to hold out, the Japanese sent reinforcements by sea, including twenty Type 95 tanks. Half of these were part of Captain Uchida's 1st Independent Tank Company, while the others were from Captain Kurobe's 2nd Independent Tank Company. These tanks were used to haul artillery across Limon Pass, a key point for controlling the island. Despite some initial successes, the Japanese tanks were gradually destroyed, and the last three were blown up during the retreat in late December.

Unfine On January 9, 1945, a massive U.S. fleet showed up in the Gulf of Lingayen, Luzon. After intense naval bombardment, the Allies established a beachhead. The Japanese, with the 2nd Tank Division, attempted to slow the Allied advance to allow other units to retreat to the mountains. The 7th Tank Regiment, led by Lieutenant Colonel Maeda, launched an attack, but suffered heavy losses in a night ambush. Despite strenuous resistance, the Japanese tanks were gradually destroyed, and Maeda died in a last desperate attack on January 27.

IWO JIMA, OKINAWA AND KURIL ISLANDS

On February 19, 1945, the United States attacked Iwo Jima, where Lieutenant Colonel Takeichi Nishi's 26th Tank Regiment was deployed with Type 97 Chi-Ha and Type 95 tanks.

Due to the rocky nature of the island, the tanks were used as armored casemates.

Despite fierce resistance, the Japanese tanks were gradually destroyed, and the island fell into Allied hands.

▲ A Japanese Ha-Go tank knocked out in Garapan (Saipan), Western Marianas.

AMPHIBIOUS TANK TYPE 2 Ka-Mi, JAPAN 1942

▲ Type 2 Ka-Mi amphibious tank built in the years 1942-44 in about 180 units.

Small photo: an amphibious tank captured during trials by members of the 2/4 Armoured Regiment at Talili Bay, Rabaul, New Britain.

AMPHIBIOUS TANK TYPE 2 Ka-Mi, JAPAN 1942

▲ Amphibious tank Type 2 Ka-Mi bare version without front and rear floating supports.

● LIGHT TANK TYPE 95 HA-GO AND DERIVATIVES

SELF-PROPELLED TANK TYPE 5 Ho-Ru, JAPAN 1945

▲ Type 5 Ho-Ru self-propelled tank: a design derived from the Type 95 Ha-Go and armed with a 47 mm Type 1 counter-tank piece.

On April 1, the United States attacked Okinawa. The Japanese garrison, supported by the 27th Tank Regiment, attempted a counteroffensive on May 4, but suffered heavy losses. Here, too, the Japanese tanks were almost all destroyed, and the regiment retreated to Shuri, where it remained until the end of May.

Finally, we also recall the Soviet attack on the Kurils.

On August 8, 1945, that is, very few days before the end of the war, the Soviet Union declared war on Japan and attacked Manchuria. Despite Japan's surrender on August 15, Soviet forces attacked Shimushu Island in the Kurils on August 18. The Japanese garrison, supported by the 11th Tank Regiment, launched a counterattack, but suffered heavy losses. After two days of fighting, hostilities ceased, and the Kurils were assigned to the Soviet Union. Even today more than 80 years after the end of the war, Japan still claims their return. The liberation of the Philippines and the subsequent battles of Iwo Jima, Okinawa and the Kurils marked Japan's final decline in World War II. Despite fierce and heroic resistance, Japanese forces were gradually overwhelmed by Allied superiority in terms of armor and strategy.

▲ A line of Ha-Go tank wrecks left in the jungle after the war. Top left: a destroyed tank of the 27th regiment on Shuri Heights in Okinawa. Right: a Japanese tank surrenders to the Australians at Rapopo.

● LIGHT TANK TYPE 95 HA-GO AND DERIVATIVES

TYPE 98A Ke-Ni, JAPAN 1942

▲ Type 98A Ke-Ni Ko (Chi-Ni) light tank, final version of the Ha-Go with increased shielding. Entered production in 1942.

LIGHT TANK TYPE 95 HA-GO AND DERIVATIVES

TYPE 98 KE-NI

The Type 98 Ke-Ni was a light tank developed by the Japanese Empire in the late 1930s as a successor to the Type 95 Ha-Go. However, its production did not start late until 1942, with World War II already underway. Equipped with a 37 mm cannon and a 7.7 mm machine gun, it did not represent a significant advancement over the Type 95, which is why its production remained limited to just over a hundred examples. No Type 98 Ke-Ni was ever used in combat, remaining stationed on Japanese metropolitan islands until the end of the war.

Development

In the late 1930s, the Japanese Imperial Army requested the design of a new light tank to replace the Type 95 Ha-Go. Competition for the vehicle involved two companies: the Mitsubishi already producing the Type 95 and the Hino Jidosha Kogyo. Both submitted their designs during 1938. The model proposed by Hino won, which was designed by a technical team that included Tomio Hara, a key figure in the development of the Japanese Army's armored forces. The tank followed a technical configuration typical of Japanese armored vehicles of the time: six load-bearing wheels on each side, grouped into three bogies, each connected to longitudinal swing arms attached to coil springs. The driving wheel was positioned in front. This version won the approval of military commands due to its superior off-road performance and received the official designation "Type 98 Ke-Ni."

Project approved, production instead encountered several problems, chief among them being the enormous fondness crews had for the Type 95 Ha-Go. Doubts also arose in the general staff, which thought it unhelpful to equip itself with too many similar models.

Hino and Mitsubishi both proceeded to produce this model, and by 1943 some 103 total were totaled. The vehicle as mentioned was holed up in remote islands and metropolitan areas where they in fact did not fire a single shot at the enemy.

Technical characteristics

The Type 98 Ke-Ni A was similar in size to the Type 95 Ha-Go, with the exception of its height, which was reduced to 1.82 meters, an advantage that made it less detectable on the battlefield. The crew always con-

TYPE 98 Ke-Ni DATA SHEET	
Dimensions	4.11 length x 2.12 width x 1.82 height (in m)
Weight	7,2 t
Crew	3 (commander/cannoneer, pilot and gunner/mechanic)
Entry and withdrawal from service	1942-1945
Fuel capacity	164 l
Engine	Mitsubishi diesel Type 100 6-cylinder, air-cooled
Maximum speed	50 km/h on road, 35 km/h off road
Autonomy	300 km, 180 km off road
Power	130 hp at 2,100 rpm
Armament	1 cannon 37mm Type 100
Secondary armament	1 Type 97 7.7 mm Arisaka machine gun
Armour	maximum of 16 mm minimum of 6 mm
Production	103 (200 according to other sources)
Users	Japanese Empire

sisted of three people: in the turret were the commander and the gunner, the latter also responsible for loading the gun. The pilot was this time positioned at the front center of the hull. The engine, located longitudinally at the side rather than at the rear, was designed to simplify and speed up maintenance operations. The tank reached a maximum speed of 50 to 55 km/h.

The armor did not undergo significant improvements over its predecessor: the maximum thickness was 16 mm, while the minimum thickness was 6 mm.

The main armament consisted of a Type 100 37-mm cannon, mounted in the center of the front of the turret, with an initial projectile speed of 760 m/s. In support was a Type 97 7.7-mm coaxial machine gun.

The total weight of the tank was 7.2 tons, 300 kg less than the Type 95. The Type 98 Ke-Ni was capable of overcoming vertical obstacles up to 0.70 meters high, fords 0.75 meters deep and trenches with a maximum width of about two meters.

▲ Definitive version of the Type 98A Ke-Ni, Japanese army light tank. Above: the version presented by Mitsubishi with four large single wheels on the tracks. Below: the anti-aircraft vehicle experiment derived from the Ke-Ni and named Type 98 28mm AA; only one prototype was produced.

TYPE 2 KE-TO

The Type 2 Ke-To was a light tank developed in Japan during World War II, a direct evolution of the Type 98 Ke-Ni (itself derived from the Type 95) and designed to replace both the latter and the now obsolete Type 95 Ha-Go. However, due to logistical and industrial difficulties in the Japanese Empire during the conflict, production remained extremely limited.

Development

In the late 1930s, the Imperial Japanese Army requested a new light tank to replace the Type 95 Ha-Go, resulting in the Type 98 Ke-Ni. Although better armed, the Type 98 still offered insufficient protection, however, as demonstrated during the early battles in the Pacific. Toward the end of 1942, new specifications were therefore issued for a more reliable and effective light vehicle capable of countering the U.S. M3/M5 Stuart tanks.

Production of the Type 2 Ke-To was delayed due to the shortage of materials and personnel that plagued the Japanese war industry as early as 1943. Started only in 1944, it proceeded slowly until the end of the war, with a total of only 29 units produced. Other sources speak of 34 units made between 1944 and 1945.

Operational deployment

Like its big brother Ke-Ni, all the Type 2 Ke-To produced also did not move from the motherland and remained in Japan, intended to counter the planned U.S. landings along with the metropolitan forces. However, the war ended before they could be deployed in combat.

An interesting aspect of the Type 2 was its design to be airborne, with the aim of providing immediate support to the Dai-1 Teishin Shūdan paratroop units or special forces. However, by the time delivery of the vehicles began, Japan was on the defensive, and even this futuristic design was abandoned.

Features

The Type 2 Ke-To was distinguished from the Type 98 mainly by its new turret, which was cylindrical in

TYPE 2 Ke-To DATA SHEET	
Dimensions	4.14 length x 2.14 width x 1.83 height (in m)
Weight	7,2 t
Crew	3 (commander/cannoneer, pilot and gunner/mechanic)
Entry and withdrawal from service	1944-1945
Fuel capacity	164 l
Engine	Mitsubishi diesel Type 100 6-cylinder, air-cooled
Maximum speed	50 km/h on road, 26 km/h off road
Autonomy	300 km, 180 km off road
Power	130 hp at 2,100 rpm
Armament	1 cannon 37 mm Type 1
Secondary armament	1 Type 97 7.7 mm Arisaka machine gun
Armour	maximum of 16 mm minimum of 6 mm
Production	29-34
Users	Japanese Empire

TYPE 2 Ke-To, JAPAN 1944

▲ Type 2 Ke-To light tank improved and latest version of the Ha-Go Type 95.

LIGHT TANK TYPE 95 HA-GO AND DERIVATIVES

shape and made entirely of cast iron, which actually increased its strength. Thanks to an improved arrangement of usable space, a Type 1 37-mm cannon could be installed, with a muzzle velocity of 800 m/s and a manual elevation of between -15° and +20°. A Type 97 7.7 mm machine gun, mounted coaxially to the gun, was intended for close defense. The commander and gunner were housed in the turret, while the tank could carry 110 shells for the cannon and 1,400 cartridges for the machine gun.

The hull was composed of armored plates fixed on spars, with maximum thicknesses of 16 mm and minimums of 6 mm with no improving variations then from the two predecessors.

The use of welding was extended, although not entirely replaced by rivets. At the front was the driver, who drove using two directional levers combined with a clutch and brake, with a manual transmission with four forward and one reverse gear. The engine, a 130-hp inline-six-cylinder Mitsubishi diesel, was located at the rear, connected to the front transmission.

The rolling train remained unchanged from the Type 98, with one front drive wheel, six double support wheels (coupled into three bogies), three double top rollers and a double idler wheel.

The steel tracks, 250 mm wide, were equipped with central lug guides.

With a total weight of 7.2 tons, the Type 2 Ke-To could reach 50 km/h on the road and cover distances of up to 190 km. On rough terrain, the speed dropped to 26 km/h. The tank also demonstrated good mobility, overcoming 0.70-meter-high vertical obstacles, trenches up to 2.10 meters wide and fords no more than 1 meter deep.

▲ Photos of the Ke-To model are extremely rare. It was a project born out of the desperation of the last months of the war and so this is also reflected in the pictures. Above: a nice view of the rear of the tank; above: a much blurrier image showing the prototype of the vehicle still missing its weapons.

TYPE 4 KE-NU, 1945

▲ Type 5 Ke-Nu command tank 19th Armoured Regiment Imperial Army - Kyushu, 1945.

LIGHT TANK TYPE 95 HA-GO AND DERIVATIVES

OTHER USERS AND EXPORT

The export of Japanese armored vehicles did not have much of a market, due to the nationalistic and aggression policy consummated against almost all neighbors and also for other reasons, with the exception of Thailand. However, after Japan's military defeat, many of these vehicles remained abandoned over a vast territory and in a levated number of countries. They were then captured and reused by many new owners.

MAIN RECIPIENTS OF EXPORT

In 1940, due to the friendly relations between Thailand and Japan, their most important partnership in the Pacific Front, 50 Type 95 tanks were delivered to the Royal Thai Army.
These relations developed into a full-fledged military alliance during World War II. The vehicles, were renamed Type 83 by the Thais, and remained in service until 1952, when they were replaced by the U.S.-supplied M24 Chaffee.
More than half of the total production of the Type 95 during the years from 1935 to the end of the World War was destined for the Chinese front. Hundreds of these tanks were abandoned by Japanese troops after Japan's unconditional surrender in the summer of 1945. Consequently, they were captured and reused by both communist and nationalist forces during the Chinese Civil War. Some of these vehicles also made their appearance in the subsequent Korean War, employed by both the PRC troops and the South Korean army.

MAIN USERS

- Japanese Empire

The operator and main recipient of tank projection for both the Imperial Japanese Army (IJA) and the Imperial Japanese Navy.

▲ A Type 83 (the Thai Ha-Go) stored at the Reserve Training Centre, Department of Territorial Defence, Bangkok.

TYPE 4 KE-NU, 1945

▲ Type 5 Ke-Nu tank of an unknown unit - Philippines, February 1945. Model equipped with the two-man turret of the Type 97 medium tank.

- Kingdom of Thailand

In 1940, the *Royal Thai Army* purchased about 50 Type 95s from Japan. Some of them led the Thai 'invasion of the Shan states of Burma during World War II, when Thailand was allied with Japan. After World War II, these tanks continued to serve with Thailand until they were decommissioned in 1952.

- Manchukuò

Some Type 95s were supplied to this their puppet ally and used for training from 1943 to 1945.

- Republic of China

Captured by Japan after the final surrender and used by the National Revolutionary Army (NRA) in the Chinese Civil War (1946 to 1949).

- People's Republic of China

Chinese Communist troops (People's Liberation Army) captured several examples from the Nationalist NRA (themselves captured from the Japanese) and received many more captured from the Soviet Union in their last fighting against Japan. They were all used in the Chinese Civil War, along with other Japanese Type 97 Chi-Ha and Type 97 Shinhoto Chi-Ha tanks . The armored force of the Chinese People's Army in 1949 numbered 349 tanks and consisted mainly of Japanese Type 95 Ha-Go and Type 97 tanks.

- Fourth French Republic

Using leftover Japanese military equipment dating back to the Japanese invasion of French Indochina, an ad hoc unit of French and Japanese armored personnel carriers (especially the 95 Go-Ha type, called the "Commando Blindé du Cambodge," was created, and this unit participated in the early stages of the First Indochina War.

▲ A line of Type 95 Ha-Go's in French service in Indochina, belonging to the French 5e RC and named respectively: Dupleix, Lyautey and Joffre!

TYPE 4 Ke-Nu, 1945

▲ Type 5 Ke-Nu tank of an unknown unit operating in Manchuria 1945.

CAMOUFLAGE AND MARKINGS

JAPANESE TANK PAINTING GUIDE

Although Japanese tanks were largely of a much inferior type far inferior to those held by the world's best powers in terms of both technology and quantity, still in 1940 Japan could boast the fifth largest armored force in the world! A due anticipation must be made regarding the often highly contradictory information available on Japanese tank camouflage in World War II.

Exact colors and how to apply them remain a complicated and confusing topic to this day. The descriptions and names of colors are not consistent among different sources.

Official instructions from the Imperial Japanese Army on how tanks were to be painted, however, are fairly well documented. But various researchers continue to debate how far the instructions were actually followed.

In summary, before 1942, the Japanese used a good variety of camouflage patterns and colors, the most common of which was a three-tone pattern with sharp outlines. On some occasions, transitions between camouflage colors were drawn with a thick black or dark gray line. Very obvious yellow stripes were also used on some vehicles. I recall that the yellow stripe was often combined with the black or dark gray contour trace between the various camouflage colors, particularly on Type 89 medium tanks. The three primary colors were khaki (Khaki-iro or called Tsuchi kusa iro), also known as "Japanese artillery brown," known in English as: Comrade Khaki (326) or Panther Yellow (210). Khaki given with very contrasting patterns that was added to mahogany brown (Tochi-iro) at about 30 percent, also called oxide red, and an olive green (Midori-iro). In some cases a fourth, darker khaki color, called "Alternative" to the basic khaki shown in the table below, was also present and used.

Officially, it was recommended that green ("kusa iro") (Army Green 342) should replace the basic khaki color ("Tsuchi kusa iro") in summer or southern operational areas. In practice, however, green was almost always used as an additional third color, accounting for about 20 percent of the vehicle area.

Beginning in 1942, the Japanese switched to a new set of colors in an attempt to better standardize their camouflage schemes. The black/dark gray outline and disruptive yellow stripes were officially abandoned. A new three-color camouflage scheme was adopted using a new khaki color similar to the dark yellow of German Panzers, which the Japanese called "dry grass" (Karekusa-iro).

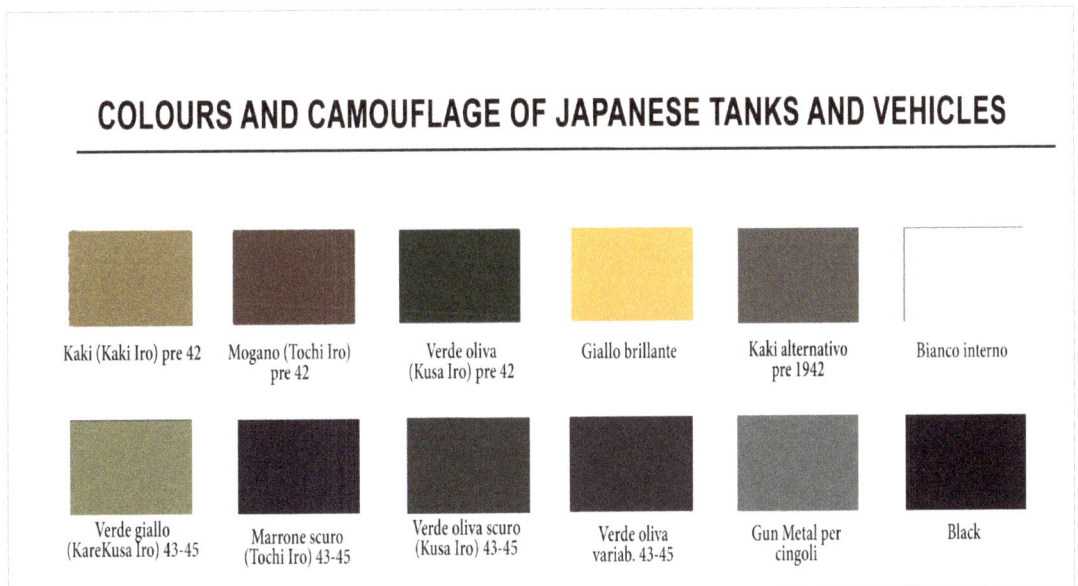

LIGHT TANK TYPE 95 HA-GO AND DERIVATIVES

The bright colors this time were a dark or monotone olive green (called Tsutikusa-iro) and a dark mahogany brown (also already known as Tochi-iro in many references, although in some cases the shade identified is darker than the pre-1942 version). In the South Pacific, an additional willow green color (Kusa-iro) was specified instead of the darker olive color. Some tank components, such as guns, also appeared to have retained the "brown artillery" color (Khaki-iro), although other regulations presented it as a slight variation of the basic khaki. Generally the camouflage patterns were stark, but from 1943 onward camouflage patterns with shaded edges became increasingly evident.

For the modeler however, it is important to remember that Japanese tanks were often not repainted with each change in regulations. It is therefore entirely acceptable to have a mix of early and late war paint schemes in the same department. Post-1942 schemes should therefore be much more common on vehicles produced from 1942 onward such as the Type 97 Kai (Shinhoto Chi-ha), some Type 95 tanks, all tanks reserved for home island defense, and the various Chi-ha-based self-propelled guns.

MODEL COLOURS FOR JAPANESE TANKS		
Color and year	Tamiya	Vallejo
Pre-1942 Khaki (Khaki-iro)	XF-49 - Khaki (90%) + XF-64 - Red Brown (10%)	Khaki 70.988 or + Green Brown 70.879
Pre-1942 Khaki (Khaki-iro) var.	XF-3 - Flat Yellow (30%) +XF64 - Red Brown (70%)	71.136 UJA Earth Brown
Pre-1942 mahogany brown (Tochi-iro)	XF-1 - Flat Black (10%) + XF-10 - Flat Brown (80%) +XF-17 (10%)	71.035 Camouflage Pale Brown
Pre-1942 Olive green (Midori-iro)	XF-26 - Deep Green	Luftwaffe Cam. Green 70.823
Yellow stripes	XF-3 - Flat Yellow	Flat Yellow 70.953
Post-1942 Khaki (Karekusa-iro)	XF-49 - Khaki	Khaki 70.988 o Middlestone 70.882
Post-1942 Brown (Tochi-iro)	XF-1 - Flat Black (10%)| XF-10 - Flat Brown (80%) + XF-17 - (10%)|	Flat Brown 70.984 o Chocolate Brown 70.872
Post-1942 Green (Tsutikusa-iro)	XF-62 - Olive Drab	Brown Violet 70.887
Post-1942 Green (Kusa-iro)	XF58 - Olive Green	Reflective Green 79.890

▲ Top view of the Ha-Go tank.

JAPANESE TANK NAMING

Most tanks used by the Imperial Japanese Army during the 1930s and 1940s were identified by two complementary designation systems. The first was used to identify all army equipment and consisted of a model number (Type) based on the imperial year in which the item was accepted or initiated. Prior to 1945, three systems of dating the year were in use in Japan: the Anno Domini system, the name of the era based on the reigning emperor's years in office, and the imperial year, which started from the then-accepted founding of Japan in 660 BCE. In 1873, the Gregorian calendar was adopted and the Japanese New Year was moved to January 1. This resulted in an alignment that combined the Western and imperial annual systems, so that 1940, for example became 2600.

Thus, until 1940/2600 the accepted practice was to use the last two numbers of the year as the type number, as in the Type 89 medium tank of 1929, with Type 100 for items accepted in 1940. After 1940 only the last digit was used, so Type 2 equipment was accepted in 1942.

The second designation system required that each tank be given a name, which was essential to distinguish two tanks accepted in the same year. At first, the names were simple: the Type 89 medium tank, for example, was "I-Go," or "first tank/model," while the Type 95 light tank was "Ha-Go," or "third tank/model."

This system was then refined to give each tank a two-letter name, where the first letter indicated the type of tank and the second the order in which the tanks were developed. Most tanks then fell into three distinct categories: Chi, Ke, and Ho, terms standing for Medium, Light, and Cannon (heavy) respectively, with Chi and Ke used as abbreviations with only one character for the extended term being: Chiu (or Chui) and Kei.

The numbering system used was somewhat abstruse by Western standards, and was based on the Iroha, a Japanese poem first mentioned in 1079. This used every character of the Japanese syllabary once, and for a long time was used to put those characters in order (in a rather poetic version of the ABC). The first two lines of the poem, transliterated into Roman letters, read:

"i ro ha ni ho he to chi ri nu ru wo"; the numbering from 1 to 12 followed:1- I o Yi, 2 - Ro, 3 - Ha, 4 - Ni, 5 - Ho, 6 - He, 7 - To, 8 - Chi, 9 - Ri, 10 - Nu, 11 - Ru, 12 - O o Wo.

▲ Replacing a 'Claw' tyre on an AB41 of the 4th Armoured Group 'Nice' stationed in Tirana, Albania. Photo taken before the Armistice. Source piciuki.com.

LIGHT TANK TYPE 95 HA-GO AND DERIVATIVES

DEFINITION AND NAMES FOR JAPANESE TANKS					
Light tanks					
Ke-Ni	Light 4	Type 98 Ke-Ni	Chi-To	Medium 7	Type 4 Chi-Ho
Ke-To	Light 7	Type 2 Ke-To	Chi-Ri	Medium 9	Type 5 Chi-Ri
Ke-Nu	Light 10	Type 4 Ke-Nu	Chi-Nu	Medium 10	Type 3 Chi-Nu
Medium tanks			**Heavy tanks**		
Chi-I	Medium 1		Ho-Io	Gun 1	Type 2 Ho-I
Chi-Ro	Medium 2	Type 89 I-Go	Ho-Ro	Gun 2	Type 4 Ho-Ro
Chi-Ha	Medium 3	Type 97 Chia-Ha	Ho-Ni	Gun 4	Type Ho.Ni
Chi-Ni	Medium 4	Never built	Ho-To	Gun 7	Type 95 120mm
Chi-Ho	Medium 5	Type 98 never built	Ho-Ri	Gun 8	
Chi-Lui	Medium 6	Type 1 Chi-He	Ho-Ru	Gun 11	Type 5 Ho-Ru

▲ Wreckage of a Ha-Go tank after the furious battle of Jwo Jima. US Signal photo. Author's colouring. Above: two images of the Type 95 model preserved at the Armoured Tank Museum in Bovington (Wiki CC1).

TYPE 95 HA-GO - MODELLISM

Model production of the Type 95 Ha-Go, and the work of Asian and European firms. The firm Dragon Models of Hong Kong leads the way. Another manufacturer is the Chinese 3D Printed also in 1/72 scale. Also on offer is the Japanese Fine Models. The only European manufacturers we have the Polish IBG, and the German MGM, which has made the model of the Type 95-derived self-propelled vehicle. All pictures belong to the catalogs of the companies mentioned.

▲ All images on this page are of models produced by Dragon Models of Hong Kong.

SELF-PROPELLED Ho-To TYPE 1 (PROTOTYPE), JAPAN 1945

▲ Prototype of a Type 1 Ho-To self-propelled vehicle derived from the Type 95. Japan 1945.

LIGHT TANK TYPE 95 HA-GO AND DERIVATIVES

▲ Above: three views of the model made by Chinese 3D Printed. ▼ Below left: a painted model made by King & Country of Hong Kong. Below right: a diorama made with the model from Japan's Fine Molds.

▲ Above: two pictures of the Type 5 Ho-Ru model by MGM, below the picture of the model box of the Type 95 Ha-Go by Polish IBG and finally the model assembled and painted by John Bond.

LIGHT TANK TYPE 95 HA-GO AND DERIVATIVES

BIBLIOGRAPHY

- S. J. Zaloga (2007) *Japanese Tanks 1939-45*, Osprey Publishing. 2007
- Ilja Moszczanski, *Typ 95 HA GO*, Wydawnictwo Militaria, Varsavia Polonia 2003
- J. Ledwoch e J. Solarz, *Czolgi Japonskie 1938-1945*, Wydawnictwo Militaria, Varsavia Polonia 2003
- T. Hara, *Japanese Combat Cars, Light Tanks and Tankettes*. Profile AFV Weapons 1973
- T. Hara, *Japanese Medium Tanks*. Profile AFV Weapons 1973
- A. Tomczyc, *Japonska Bron Pancerna- Japanese armor vol. 1,2,3 e 4 Tank Power* by AJ Press Polonia 2002
- R. Cansière, *USMC M4A2 Sherman vs Japanese Type 95 Ha-Go*. Osprey Duel serie 2021
- P. Chamberlain and C. Ellis (1967), *Light Tank Type 95 Kyu-go*, Profile Publication.
- D. McCormack *Japanese Tanks and Armoured Warfare 1932-45* Casemate 2021
- G. Rottman *World War II Japanese Tank Tactics* Bloomsbury Publishing 2011
- AA.VV Japanese *Armor in World War 2* AK Interactive
- A. M. Tomczyk (2002) *Japanese Armor vol.2* Aj-Press.
- A. M. Tomczyk (2002) *Japanese Armor vol.9* Aj-Press
- A. M. Tomczyk (2002) *Japanese Armor vol.10* Aj-Press
- D. Nešić, (2008), *Naoružanje Drugog Svetskog Rata-Japan*, Beograd
- A. Ludeke, *Waffentechnik Im Zweiten Weltkrieg*, Parragon.
- P. Trewhitt (2000) *Armored fighting vehicles*, Grange Book.
- *Japanese tank and antitank warfare*, Military Intelligence Service. 1945
- *Japanese Tanks and Tactics*, Military Intelligence Service.
- *Japanese Tank units*" Maru Magazine 7/2013
- *Japanese Tanks on Pacific Islands*" Maru Magazine 2/2013

PUBLISHED TITLES

TWE-037 EN

www.ingramcontent.com/pod-product-compliance
Ingram Content Group UK Ltd.
Pitfield, Milton Keynes, MK11 3LW, UK
UKHW060216240426
12048UKWH00030BB/1694